'...that was wicked wot they done 'bout that Chapel

A Cratfield Miscellany

by

Chrissie Kitchen

Edited by Nigel Cousins

2019

First Edition

Published and Printed by

Leiston Press

Masterlord Industrial Estate

Leiston

Suffolk

IP16 4JD

Telephone Number: 01728 833003

Email: glenn@leistonpress.com

ISBN 978-1-911311-47-8

© Chrissie Kitchen

All rights reserved. No part of this book may be reproduced, stored in a retrieval system, or transmitted in any form or by any means electronic, mechanical, photocopying, recording or otherwise, without the prior permission of the author.

Introduction and Acknowledgements

I was born in Germany. My family moved to Laxfield when I was five. I was schooled in Laxfield and Stradbroke Modern. I have lived in Cratfield for over thirty years.

Cratfield seemed to me the only local village without a publication about it. I wanted to put that right. I have been formulating the idea for some years, but I am one hundred per cent prehistoric when faced with technology. Nigel Cousins has been very helpful in enabling me to finalise the content and go to press. I thank him for reading and editing my scrawl. I should like to give a special mention to his long-suffering wife, Anne.

I thoroughly enjoyed having a mardle with all the characters interviewed. I felt proud to be able to record their voices. I am delighted to present the village with this little book. I hope people from Cratfield and beyond will enjoy reading it.

All proceeds from its sale will be divided equally between the Church and the Village Hall.

Chrissie Kitchen

In tribute to my three children
Sallyanne, Darren, Louise, and their families

In memory of my late dear brother Michael 1950-2006

A little book for Cratfield

The remotest of places

Approached via single green lanes across quiet rolling countryside, often bare and moated by ditches, sometimes winding, with walls of ancient hedgerow – under vast and shifting Suffolk skies – Cratfield can seem the remotest of places. Yet people have found a home here for centuries.

Cratfield Voices

In these pages you can find out more about the people of Cratfield and its history. The first part, **Cratfield Voices**, was compiled from interviews and creates a vivid picture of times when there were pubs and shops in the village. Water had to be pumped out of the ground by windmills – a good night out was a trip to Halesworth on a little blue bus, a night at the pictures and a fish and chip supper. There are memories of American airmen during the war. People talk fondly and with regret about the Congregational Chapel that was demolished. Its cemetery remains - graves still faithfully tended.

A Miscellany

The second part is a miscellany based on documents, everything from the Domesday Book to the Parish Records. Find out about the history of some of Cratfield's more notable old houses. Learn about the Cratfield murder in 1793 – so shockingly brutal that it became notorious throughout England. Discover the source of the annoying creaking noise heard on Silverleys Green in 1959.

Nigel Cousins

Cratfield Voices

John and Pam Brown

John Brown

'Everyone came to the top of our drive for water... Them days are gone.'

John is keen to talk about the old times, having combed his hair and put on his best clothes for the occasion. He sits by the fire and sips tea as he talks in Suffolk tones.

The fate of the Congregational Chapel

'Mother made us go to Chapel and Church too. Twice on Sundays. The Chapel was built 30th September 1812 and demolished in the 1960s. Reverend J.C. Salisbury M.D. was appointed Pastor there for 25 years, resigned in 1855. Retired and built Salisbury house.

'It was a large old building with galleries, pretty stained-glass windows and lovely brass oil lamps that were lowered by a chain to light. It was kept warm by a large black coal burning stove.

'At harvest time a small room at the back of the building was used to sell produce. Suppose that room was the chapel of rest really. Toilets were out the back - bucket and chuck it! There was no flush toilets in them days. As a teenager, I used to keep the yard clean of weeds. Tidy it and keep it nice. Paid £20 a year, later my cows kept the grass down.

'Will Sillett was the undertaker. A man by the name of Woodland was the Sunday School teacher. Can't remember what I learned. Woodland helped us boys keep the yard free of weeds. We think he was scared of his wife as he would stand behind a gravestone and have a puff! Good ole boy he was.

'A petition was launched to save the chapel from demolition but that weren't any good. That still happened.' John shrugs.

'The rubble was taken to Linstead Farm and the tiles are on a house in this village to this day. The font went to Stowmarket Congregational

I believe. Some of the settles from the chapel are in the Village Hall Cratfield. Halesworth demolition gang had the doin's of it Minns by name. The railings were made of iron and ran all the way around the building all went [years before] for the war effort. The place seated 300 folks. Another chapel on Silverley's Green looked like an upturned funnel, with two large doors on the front they sang Sankey hymns … they took that down too.'

Repairing St Mary's Church

Farming was John's life, but he turned his hand to other things as country people do. He helped his uncle William Bailey with his building business around the area. He worked on church repairs. William Bailey kept an immaculate account book which contains the details of the extensive building work he did in the local area. John Brown helped repairing the church and was a pallbearer.

Here's an example taken from William Bailey's account book for 1972:

St Mary's Church Cratfield

Stripping slates splines off the roof cleaning up the splines etc cleaning the beams and rafters.

Hours of work

J Sillett   32 hours

J Brown   32 "

W Brown   32 "

 E Rees   6 "   @£2-20 per hour

'The water was crystal clear'

John can remember the days when there was no piped water in Cratfield. 'Everyone came to the top of our drive for water - we had a bore and windmill. People would arrive with buckets and water drums on wheels. The water was crystal clear. Them days are gone.'

Sadly, he died in 2015.

Pam Brown

A farming life

Pam relates the story of Bell Farm and her husband's family. In 1906 Mr John Brown moved to **the Bell**, Cratfield. He ran it as a pub alehouse. It was owned by Lacons Brewery from Gt Yarmouth. John Brown's son George Brown married Elsie Bailey who lived at The Forge Cratfield. John Brown and his wife then moved to the Almshouse next to the church with their other son. George had three children – John (who married Pam), Elsie and Noel. He bought the Bell from Lacons with the land - 26 acres

John and Pam had a bungalow built on the stackyard next to the Bell. Pam sighs that it took six years to save the money to build the home. It cost £12,000. They brought up their three children there:

Tracy, Paul and Trevor.

Pam reminds us of some of the hardships of rural life saying that there was no electricity until the 50s'.

'John would milk by hand'

'John had a herd of Jersey cows starting with eight and at the finish there were about 30.

'The cows were turned out on Dawson's meadow which we still own. A footpath runs diagonally across and is used frequently. Footpaths were so important as there was very little transport and farmers took the shortest route and children walked to the village school.'

Pam smiles. 'We used to walk the herd to our other meadow next down the road. I used to walk in front with balls of string tying up the entrance to people's houses to avoid the cows from entering. Then I walked behind on the way back unravelling the string ready for the next time. John would milk by hand. The milk then went through an apparatus like a wash basin cooler, before emptying into churns. The churns would then be carried to the top of the drive ready for the lorry to take them to United Dairies at Halesworth train station.

'John would calve, and if a cow was in difficulty, he would master it roll his sleeve up and deliver. All cows were artificially inseminated. The calves would then be collected and sold on to market. He was a quiet man of few words, but it has been said John was an amazing asset, helping neighbouring farms when their herds were in trouble.'

Brian and Gwendoline Cole

'Father had a few guns all loaded propped against the wall in the kitchen.'

A chat with Brian Cole and his wife Gwendoline is enjoyable and revealing. Brian Cole was one of three children born at Poplar Farm, Silverley's Green. He started school in Cratfield, moving to Laxfield when the school was closed. He went to Secondary School in Stradbroke. Brian's early school memories include the cruelty of the teacher who would hit you across the knuckles, drawing blood. One child had an accident in class and was forced to sit in it.

Dad's Army

Brian likes to tell stories about the Home Guard. His dad, Ted, was in it. One day he was practising presenting arms in the farmhouse kitchen somewhat over enthusiastically – the rifle barrel ended up going through the ceiling, 'Darn great hole it made too!' says Brian.

'Headquarters was a tin hut outside Cleaveland's shop - **The Poacher**. Oil lamps were used and left the Home Guards with black faces. One day a fleet of aircraft were flying overhead. The shop owner thought it funny to drop a brick from an upstairs window onto the tin roof. We fell over each other trying to get out. Father would laugh at the TV programme **Dad's Army** - it was just like that every bit of it.'

Medical matters

'When I was a boy I complained of pains in my stomach, Mother said we had better get to the Doctor at Fressingfield. We cycled. I could hardly push the pedals. It was an abscess on my appendix. I was in the hospital for weeks.

'The same Doctor had a large loud voice. He asked a patient to bring in a sample of water on his next visit.' The patient obeyed his instructions to the letter. The voice of the exasperated medic boomed throughout the surgery on the patient's next visit:

"I meant a sample of piss, not tap water!"

'The same Doctor was partial to a little drop of drink. Once, when visiting me at home he blundered into the stair rail – in so doing, pulled the banister off the walls loudly complaining - "Confounded thing!"'

In a farming household in the past was not unusual to have a small home arsenal casually arranged in the home.

'Father had a few guns all loaded propped against the wall in the kitchen. One day I thought I would shoot a rabbit. Mother replaced the gun with the others. When Dad went to use the same gun, quickly grabbing it, fired and no bullet. Mother hadn't reloaded it.'

Vicar turns a blind eye

Brian has fond memories of Leslie Hipkins, the vicar, even though he was christened at the chapel because his mother was not so keen on the vicar.

'The vicar, Leslie Hipkins at the time, was very good to me. Let's say he saw me doing something I should not have been doing … I had a word with him and explained why.'

Mr Hipkins helpfully turned a blind eye.

Robin Bryenton

'Them days are gone more's the pity.'

A mardle with Robin Bryenton gives a great insight into old times.

He was born in a little cottage beside the village school in School Lane, Cratfield. He attended the school from age five to nine. He remembers Mrs Jolly as the one and only teacher and also her son, Desmond.

The school chums he recalls were Dougie Keable, Ralph and John Stannard, Dennis Moulton, Billy and Eileen Moulton. There was Hazel, Rodney and Shelia Brenton. He recalls John Mills, Aubrey 'Ike' Ward and Noel Brown.

Robin remembers a train set arranged around the class room. 'It was a highlight marvellous, truly wonderful.'

Like other ex-pupils Robin remembers school dinners with great pleasure. 'Mrs Lewry was the cook and her meals were delicious, great cook.'

'I used to fetch water from for the family with a yoke and two pails.'

Robin scatters a few more memories into the conversation.

'I worked at Manor Farm as a stock man on Mill Road now Huntingfield Road. Down this road was a field full of orchids that was sight to see.

'Mr Armstrong had a shop top of church road that sold eggs, bootlaces and bacon.

'In 1944 a bomb exploded on Metfield airdrome that shook a lot of houses in Cratfield and blasted off the back of an aircraft.

'There was a pond where Mr Cleaveland had a shop [what was the **Poacher**]. It was filled in around the early sixties. I used to fetch water from for the family with a yoke and two pails.

'The now demolished Congregational Chapel was a playground for us children - running around the gallery, charging up the stairs three or four at a time Great brass oil lamps hung from the ceiling. Shame that had to go.

'We had fun picking blackberries and hips then got a few pennies for them. Them days are gone, mores the pity.'

Julian Askew
'...doing what I jolly well like'

Julian is married to Barbara and has lived in Cratfield for 10 years. His life has all been in farming. He considers he has had 'a pretty good life all in all.'

He was born and brought up on a farm in Grundisburgh. He was privately educated at Langley School, Loddon. After Agricultural College in Writtle he worked for years as an Estate Manager.

He married in 1965 – four years after his beloved 1961 Austin A30 first hit the road.

He retired to Cratfield. In his time, he has seen people come and go, houses built, and a pub shut. He remembers his upbringing as being rather grim – 'Victorian, no freedom.'

This is in marked contrast with his life now.

'My hobby is drawing, sketching and doing what I jolly well like,' he laughs.

Ralph Creasey
'...farming in their DNA'

Ralph Creasey's family have farming in their DNA. They have farmed locally for many generations. In Cratfield they owned Linstead Farm, The Firs, Holly Tree Farm, Moat Farm and Holly Tree Farm.

Noah's Gifts

Ralph's great-great-great-grandfather Noah bought Cratfield Hall. Noah thought a great deal of Cratfield. To show his thankfulness when he recovered from an illness in 1902, he paid for two windows to be installed St Mary's Church. One was in the chancel and one near the organ.

Wall Street Crash

Ralph likes to tell the story of Noel, a family member who moved to Florida. He was living and working on a citrus farm at the time of the Wall Street Crash. In the ensuing chaos the farm went bust. Noel had the chance to buy the land for a song but couldn't afford the tax. Leaving behind a potentially lucrative future farming in Florida he had to pack his bag and head towards the sunset. He remained in America but left farming. He retrained as a butler – of all things – and lived the rest of his life in Boston.

Ralph, who is married with two children, still farms over in Metfield.

Ted Greenard

'Having to swallow cod liver oil and rose syrup…urggh!'

Ted was born Edward Albert Greenard. His mother was a midwife and his father, Frederick, served in the Royal Fusiliers in France and Belgium. Later he was in the Home Guard in Cratfield. Ted visited French, Belgium and also Germany, courtesy of the military when he did National Service.

Ted remembers having to go to Sunday school at the Congregational Chapel Sunday mornings with the Reverend van Hooten and Mrs Gladys Wink, the Sunday school teacher.

'I went to school here in the village along with John Brown and Kenny Girling.'

He recalls being subjected to a good old-fashioned health care routine as a child. 'Having to swallow cod liver oil and rose syrup…urggh!

'We used to have fun making slides on the Heveningham Hall lake, sliding with hobnailed boots on. We had fun making catapults from hazel.'

"Hey mister have you got a sister?"'

'Of course, I was only a lad but remember the Irish and the Americans when they were stationed here. Quite frequently – alternate weekends – a fight would ensue after the pub, the **Bell** or the **Jolly Farmers**. Bare-knuckle scrap. All friendly, that's all.

'Dad grew vegetables and the Yanks loved them they would call out, "Hey Pop have you got any cucumbers or tomatoes?" They would eat them as they were. On the Metfield aerodrome, us lads would love to see the Liberators, machine guns, Thunderbolts.

'Sadly, there was a crash. A Beaufort plane was shot down with nine fatalities. It was trying to fly back to the drome. Everyone did what they could to keep the wings up.'

Ted's final memory of the American Servicemen in the War is an abidingly cheeky one.

'I can hear them now - "Hey mister, have you got a sister?"'

Donald Edward High
'They was good them days - moi hat they was.'

Donald Edward High was born on Mills Farm Laxfield 1940.

'Aunt May Nessling delivered me. Everyone called her Aunt. Also laid folk out.'

His upbringing was really rural. He recalls milking cows with Queenie Dyer and Hazel Fleet by hand at Manor Farm Laxfield which was owned by Fred Johnson.

'a good ole boy'

Donny worked for many years delivering coal for Moyes coal merchant taking sacks of coal to households as far as Southwold. Once he was delivering coal to a place near the lighthouse in Southwold. Donny remembers a gentleman approaching him and asking him,

"Yar a High aren't yer?"

"Yes. I am Donny High." said Donny.

The gentleman replied, 'I knowed yar Granfer in Wingfield. Sold me rats, rabbits, pheasants, ferrets all for 2/6d – well after a little he says, "You can hev 'em for nuthin'." He was a good ole boy.'

Adventures of the Peewit Patrol

But the best fun of all was being in the Boy Scouts. Donny loved it and still enjoys talking about the fun they had in the Peewit Patrol. He recalls that they went camping 'as far away as Homersfield.'

'We cycled there and back. Didn't think nothin' of it. Them was good ole days,' he chuckles.

He lists the names of his fellow scouts. 'There was Karl Easy, Michael Hamm, Rex Howlett. The Scout Masters were Mr Charles Sparrow the shop keeper from Sparrows of Laxfield, and Mr. Maine from Green Farm Ubbeston .'

They camped at Heveningham Hall at weekends. They camped in Laxfield Woods. A man named Jimmy Bye used to live near there. Donny says he used to sing, "Can yer make a rabbit poi?"

'They was good them days - moi hat they was. We had three tents. We cooked on an open fire. Tea in a billy can. Joints of meat in a biscuit tin. Canvas bucket for the water. Milk cans from the farm. We sang **Ging Gang Goolie** and **John Brown's Body Lies a Mould'rin' in the Grave**.

The Scouts were called The First All Saints Church Group. The boys from the Chapel were desperate to join but their parents were too strict. Perhaps they feared their little angels would be led astray.

As Donny vividly puts it, 'Chapel boys wanted to join the Scouts. Parents refused. "Sunday saint, weekday devil," that was what they said.'

Tubby Revell

'... that was wicked wot they done 'bout that Chapel.'

Tubby is happy to share some reminiscences about Cratfield. All told in the richly evocative tones of a proud Suffolk man.

Tubby Revell was born in 1920 in Tye Cottage Cratfield. His brother and sisters were Gordon, Florence, Hilda and Maddy

'I was named after my father, Sydney Victor. I was delivered at home; we all were in those days.'

'We did spy on folks what nivver drew thar curtains!'

He smiles as he recalls some of the things he got up to as a boy with his friends.

'We was really naughty all on us.

'We did spy on folks what nivver drew thar curtains!

'We used ter swim in the pond with nuthin' on. Cor yeah, we runned away with some of the gals' clothes.'

Tubby was at the village school. The teachers he remembers were Miss Jolly, and Miss Hadingham, who, quite typically for the time, had a rather cruel nickname: 'She sorta limped, we called her Strider.'

'Miss Hadingham took us boys on the 'llotment plots. She showed me how ter grow turnips, sprouts, runner beans, chickens and lettuce.

'Cor she was somethin' fierce. But boy, she knew how ter grow things.'

His brother Gordon was incorrigible. 'My brother Gordon, he's a one. He hurled a whole wheelbarra in the pond.'

Tubby says that they all got blamed for it. But it did not stop him from being successful at growing vegetables. 'Oi still won all the prizes that oi did for moi veg.' Miss Hadingham's lessons had clearly not been in vain.

A note for the teacher

Tubby recalls with laughter one time when he was off school with a bad stomach and diarrhoea. His Mother, no great letter writer, found it very hard to write a polite note to the teacher.

'When I was orf school once with a tummy upset my mum sent a note saying why I weren't at school but couldn't spell it. She was a puffin' and gettin' in a state 'bout that note.' In the end, 'She writ oi had the shits. Can't get plainer than that, can yer?'

During the war there was an influx of American servicemen. But the Brown family, local publicans, retained the respect of the locals by making sure that not all the beer went to the thirsty Americans.

'Brown family roight nice people they was, wouldn't let them Yanks hev all the beer. The landlord wouldn't let 'em drink all on it. Saved it for us boys, that he duzzy well did.'

Tubby shows some regret when he talks about the demolition of the local Congregational Chapel. It had been built in 1811. The quite extensive burial ground is still to be seen. 'Dear, that was wicked wot they done 'bout that Chapel. Mr. Vincent went to help sort it out, but they still pulled it down. Bloody well wicked, but that's done now.'

'...enough to make a cat laugh...'

If the fate of the Chapel makes him rueful, he talks with amusement and fun about a less august building which is still standing now. Our Village Hall.

'Mr Rogers had the Hut built. On 'Hut Road '[Manse Lane]. We boys watched it bein' built. That come as a Flat Pack. We had many a game playing crawling underneath to see who come out first. 1929 that was built. When they was a building that we watched that go up. That was enough to make a cat laugh, honestly.

'Mrs. Rogers thought a lot of me. Doddy little ole woman, she was. She wore a brooch, a pink dragonfly. We played a trick on her. Knocked on her door. When she opened it, a plank o' wood fell in.

'We had a galot o fun in the Hut. Parties and concerts, plays – **Murder in the Red Barn** was one of them. Victor Vincent used to sing when he come from the army. My nephew Eric Mayhew and his wife Dot used to run dances in the 70's, Country and Western they called 'em, and raised lots of money for good causes in the Cratfield Hut.'

A night out in Halesworth

Tubby enjoyed trips to Halesworth – there were buses in those days!

'Have you heard of Naylor's Buses? That was blue and all on us used to git on that fer outings - pictures in Halesworth, fish and chips arterwards. Lovely them days were. Holidays were spent in Southwold and around.'

Tubby worked at various local jobs. He worked as a cowman for Creasey's at Linstead Farm. He worked on the Mobbs family farm. He has been a grave digger and a coal merchant delivering coal from Laxfield train station depot.

Cratfield was not without its racy side: 'Silky Tie used to come around selling door to door. Sold ties with naked gals on 'em. Quite nice they was. Sorta wide at the bottom.'

One last gently mischievous snapshot from Tubby's memories of long ago.

'One snowy winter's night us boys we had had enough beer into us at **The Bell**. That was a snowin' hard. We was all on push bikes. S'pose we were all messing around with snowballs singing and laughing. There was a p'liceman a-shoutin' at us ter git home, making all that row. We dropped our bikes and runned as fast as we could, slipping around the road. When one of us turned around to see the p'liceman he was on his back arse up'ards waving his fists. We could not stop laughing. I do believe some on us wet ourselves.'

Jack Symonds

From Cratfield to Hiroshima and back

He was born on 4th September 1924 at Pear Tree Cottage North Green Cratfield. Jack's father, also called Jack, bought the cottage for £90 in 1924.

Jack was born at a time when Cratfield lacked electricity and flushing toilets – drinking water had to be pumped out of the ground. It was the year the Zeppelin made its first transatlantic flight and Marlon Brando was born. Mrs Greenard the midwife delivered Jack, and he jokingly used to say that she was, 'The first to smack my bottom, and definitely not the last.'

He was christened John but as two boys at school had the same name he was always known as Jack.

He attended Cratfield School until he was 14 and a half and then went to work at Cratfield Hall.

In August 1943 aged 19 Jack was called up for National Service and headed off to Great Malvern for Naval training to serve as a gunner aboard defensively equipped merchant ships. He sailed aboard *HMS Queen Elizabeth* from Scotland to New York, where he and 11 others took control of the newly built Liberty Ship *SS Samtay*. Liberty Ships were specially and rapidly built in the war to carry cargo to Britain.

A visit to Hiroshima

Jack visited many countries and ports, but one place left him with a lasting impression. In 1946, in a letter to his mother, he talks about a visit to Hiroshima that took place only nine months after the first atomic bomb had been dropped in the bombing of Japan. Jack collected a bottle and a pair of scissors that had been melted by the blast and which are still in his collection today.

Jack would laugh and say he travelled the world and never owned a passport – 'Try doing that today', he would say. For his War Service Jack was awarded The Atlantic Star, The Italy Star, The Burma Star and the 1939- 45 Star medals. His family were very proud.

A family home

He built his family home mostly by himself. He crafted his own breeze blocks and fitted his own kitchen, cutting up old bomb boxes to make the parquet flooring. He grew vegetables, kept animals and honey bees.

Jack is no longer with us, so many thanks to grandson Mark for allowing access to the tribute he wrote to his grandfather.

Roy Vincent
'I told 'em I was eighteen 'cos there was nothing to do round here'.

Roy Vincent was born in Fressingfield. When the family had to move, Roy recalls having to get on his bike and pedal round the local area helping Alfred, his father, find somewhere to live. That's how they came to Cratfield.

Alfred Vincent bought a shop in the centre of Cratfield from a Mr Owles for £743. He bought the neighbouring two cottages for £390. Roy's father sold one of them to a newlywed couple. Roy remembers them as paying £25 every six months by way of a mortgage. Because the cottages were thatched, they fell into disrepair. Roy's father engaged Bill Bailey (a local builder) to replace the rooves with tiles from the Congregational Chapel bought for a penny halfpenny each.

'he got gangrene right bad'

Alfred had fought in the battle of the Somme at the Western Front. He was a sniper in the trenches. Roy says, 'He got gangrene right bad and had to come home, but lost one leg, then the other.' He must have had enough of war – when the Second World War came around, Roy recalls, his father did not want to be in the Home Guard.

National Service

In the fifties it was time for Roy to do his National Service. Roy recalls being seventeen when he joined the Army. He lied about his age, 'I told 'em I was eighteen 'cos there was nothing to do round here.'

Roy says, 'When I was a lad of fourteen, I damaged my eye with a catapult. I drew it back and bang the bloody thing flew into my eye and I've had trouble ever since.'

Despite this, the Army took him. His vision was passed as being Grade 2 A. He joined the Royal Electrical and Mechanical Engineers and served in Devon and later in Worcester.

Because he was good with a scythe the Army gave him the job of keeping the nettles down on the cricket pitch. Whilst in the REME there was a wet summer and Roy got a letter from Captain Webb to allow him to return to Cratfield for three weeks to help with the harvest.

Sam never paid him back

Roy would earn a bit of extra money cleaning the officers' mess. He collected empty bottles – at the time you were paid 2d for every bottle you returned. This was quite a money spinner – he says his pockets were soon full of money which he carried back to Cratfield with him. He took it all home apart for two shillings and sixpence which he lent to Sam McCready from Liverpool. Roy ruefully remember to this day that Sam never paid him back.

In the old days there was a railway line between Cratfield and Laxfield. Roy remembers the name of the Engine Driver as being Frankie Bloom. At one time Roy and his mate Wag Stokes were employed to cut down hedges for a proposed extension to the line. The railway company even started to lay cinders – but the line never got built. The railway line closed in 1952.

Tom and Sheila Webster
'I loathed school. Simply hated it.'

When they get talking Sheila and Tom are full of memories recalling times when things were different to how they are nowadays.

The shadow of war

Thomas Walter Robert Webster was born into a farming family. In 1939 they moved to Elm Lodge on Chippenhall Green, Fressingfield. The storm clouds gathering over Europe cast a dark shadow even in rural Suffolk. Tom's sister Edith was promised a birthday party – but only if war was not declared. September 2nd, the day of the party came, Britain was still at peace, so Edith had her party. It was just as well for the next day at 11.15 BST Neville Chamberlain announced that the deadline for the German withdrawal for troops from Poland had expired and that Britain was at war with Germany.

Tom was a boarder at Langley School, Loddon, Norfolk – which some might consider having offered a better grade of education than could have been obtained locally. The young Tom did not think so.

'I loathed school. Simply hated it. Couldn't wait to leave. It's just me. I am afraid I loathed it all. I left school and went straight into farming. Mixed in farming, we called it, with a house cow.'

In 1955 Tom married Sheila in Cratfield Church. They had three children. They still love their home.

Sheila says, 'Tom, this house is so lovely, standing just so on the common with all the beauty of wild flowers – and those pyramidal orchids.'

'Yes.' Tom chips in, 'So cosy inside on winter's evenings too.'

'I loved being read to'

Sheila, Tom's wife, and her siblings Hazel and Rodney were born in Cratfield in a house opposite the Village Hall. All three attended the village school.

Sheila recalls, 'A Miss Jolly was the head and only teacher.' She remembers doing country dancing – partly because, as she had no sense of rhythm, it was not a favourite pastime.

'The class was led out to the playground; Miss Jolly having carried out the wind-up gramophone. Then country dancing would commence – as near as we knew how!

'Mrs Lewry was the cook, wonderful cook too. Mrs Lewry was an Irish woman. She started by cooking for the Irish workers that lived where the Knox family now live.

'Inside the classroom Miss Jolly would keep attention by reading Oliver Twist and all the classics. I loved being read to.'

When time came to leave the village school, Sheila and Hazel went to Sir John Leman School and Rodney (along with Roy Vincent, whose story is also in this book) went to Bungay Grammar. But pretty soon to make the travelling from Cratfield easier all the children were sent to the same school.

'We journeyed by taxi and then caught the train from Halesworth.' All three children achieved O Levels.

The shops that Cratfield has lost

Nowadays, Cratfield has lost its pub and there are no shops of any kind left. Not so in those days.

There were shops, including a tailors' and a dressmaker. Just by recalling the bits that she could remember, Sheila conjures up a Cratfield much different from today – more self-sufficient, with more people of working age with families. Human memory is less cut and dried than official records but is infinitely more vivid and Sheila's memories summon up another world.

'A beautiful dress with covered buttons'

Sheila recalls 'A Miss Clarke lived at Bell View – a shop dress maker and tailor, with her family. Her dressmaking skills were divine.'

Sheila glowingly recalls one very special item. 'A beautiful dress with covered buttons. Perfect. I loved it.'

'John Brown [an old Cratfield neighbour] remembers the tailor sitting in the window cross-legged and sewing. Miss Clarke made wedding dresses bridesmaids' dresses too. Miss Clarke lost her husband during the war.

'The Post Office used to be at the local shop – Mr and Mrs Cleaveland – it was across the road at the front of Appleacre. Later the shop was run by Mr and Mrs Mobbs and Mr Vincent also had the shop.

'Years later the Post Office returned to the shop [later it became the **Cratfield Poacher**, now it is a private house]. Tradesmen and amenities have disappeared along with the times. Things change. John Lewis opened the bar. He owned the **Poacher** at the time with his family, so it became a shop and pub. Sometime in the eighties Mr and Mrs Barker reopened the Post Office and extended the bar.'

'sweets and string bootlaces'

'A Mr Armstrong owned the little shop at the top of Church Hill selling such things as sweets and string bootlaces. Also, a Mr, Taylor owned the shop at one point – he sold cigarettes sweets. This was also run by a Mr Osborne.

'Mr Baily used the premises for his building work shop and store. The building was demolished and in its place a cottage was built. Probably in the nineties.

'Mrs Sillett lived at Post Office cottages, now Bell Green cottage. Mrs Sillett was the Post Mistress along with George Brown for many, many years. Something like 65 years between them. Both retired when postal vans were introduced.'

Sheila recalls, 'Dora Frost was responsible for the Parish Magazine. The

Mill on Chippenhall Green was demolished in 1936. The **Jolly Farmers** pub closed in the early 60's.' It lay between Cratfield and Fressingfield.

Sheila remembers having to carry a pint of beer very carefully back to the house on the Green for a special visitor who they thought might be thirsty. It was a tricky job. It was also a waste of time as it stood all afternoon untouched – the visitor did not want to drink ale.

Satan Jack

There were some rare characters in those days. Sheila recollects Satan Jack. Others knew him as Turpentine Jack. Tom remembers him living on Silverley's Green. He remembers his dwelling being a rough corrugated shed covered in a tarpaulin and straw. It's a mystery as to what his real name was and what he did for a living. Tom believes his name might have been Jack Sheldrake. It would be great if anyone reading this could cast any light on this eccentric local resident.

Dead Man's Lane

Every country place in England has strange or evocative names for its lanes and byways. When asked how Dead Man's Lane got its sinister name, Tom Webster's thoughts were:

'I remember flowers being left at the spot where a shepherd boy was murdered - perhaps he was a gypsy. All this happened 1700 or thereabouts.'

Shelia remembers attending the Congregational Chapel, which was closed in 1945. Now, sadly, demolished. Time has passed, the building is long gone, but memories are vivid.

'On the Congregational Chapel Anniversaries, we all had something new or different to wear. I had a lovely golden bridesmaid's dress. My mother recycled this garment by removing the frilly hem and proceeded to decorate the hat with this – I had to wear it of course. For this occasion, we were all given texts to read out aloud. My mother didn't agree with the contents of this text and gave me another to read. No one noticed.'

Sheila remembers one Harvest Festival at the Chapel. 'Mr Mouser had a large tall pear tree, it is still there at Clear View. Mr Mouser filled his wheelbarrow up with these pears then pushed it all the way to the chapel from Silverley's Green for the Thanksgiving.'

The ghost of Linstead Hall

Sheila also talks of a haunted house in Linstead. She seems convinced, though Tom remains sceptical and passes no comment.

'Mr Sam Webster, Tom's father, visited his daughter Edith at Linstead Hall. Violet, Sam's wife, had not been too well of late so decided to stay in bed at Linstead Hall. The house is believed to be of Tudor origin with a Queen Ann front. Mr Webster sat alone in the lounge area one evening when he heard the door open, and a woman drifted through. Assuming it was his wife he said, "Hello you must be feeling better." No answer. The woman disappeared through a closed door. On no account was my father in law imaginative.

'When his wife recovered, he related the tale a of seeing a middle-aged woman with quite a full figure, "Well really how can you mistake me for the thing you saw?" said the Violet, indignant at the suggestion that she might be in any way on the large side.'

Others who have lived at Linstead Hall have strange stories and sightings too!

Cratfield Miscellany
From the annals of the Parish Council

Another way of accessing Cratfield's past is by trawling through the minutes of Parish Council meetings. Here are some snippets of what was once red-hot news, and possibly red-hot gossip, for Cratfieldians.

Ivy Cottages, the Oak Family

Cratfield United 1954 - 55

School Boys School Allotment, Tubby Revell Front, Centre Samuel Wilson

Cratfield Harvest

Chippenhall Mill, Joyce Creasy, Madge Sillett, Norah Creasy December 1929

Cratfield Post Office, P. Cleveland

Coronation Street Procession, Cratfield May 1937.
Anne & Yvonne Creasy, Pauline Salmon & Mary Manning in front top picture.
Also in the photos is Winnie Vincent from the shop and a boy called Russell.
Pauline Salmon was the policeman's daughter.

Pickfed Hill, Cratfield. Heavy Snowfall

Boys on the Allotment

P.C. Herbert Read and his Wife Rosa (Nee Mizon) and Son Herbert who also grew up and spent many years as a Suffolk Police Officer. During their stay in Cratfield, on the 11th March 1915, the youngest of their two Daughters was born, Edna Thora Nunn (Nee Read). Edna lives in Lowestoft at the grand age of 92 years. Thora as she likes to be known, occasionally visits the "Cratfield Poacher" for Lunch, and always receives a hearty welcome from mine hosts.

Cratfield Store is now the Poacher. The door has been filled in. George Browns father bought the Bell. The John Brown's Grandson ran the pub with family until it closed in 1957. May Sillet lived in Post Office Cottages next door to the pub, now Whipple Tree Cottage. Both retired after 65 years of service. Vans were introduced and bicycles were made redundant.

Size isn't everything – but it's important

November 24th, 1937

The clerk reported that, owing to an error through the boundary posts being pulled up, one allotment at 9 shillings was charged to Henry Girling instead of Derrick Girling. Derrick Girling claimed he hired the land as one and a half acres instead of one and three quarters. The council agreed to forego the rent of 1 shilling for 1937.

The council on the proposal, Mr Algar seconded by Mr Webster, agreed that the allotment field be properly measured afresh with posts to mark each allotment.

Wanted – Pied Piper for Cratfield

February 29th, 1940

Devastation of rats to arrange person to take charge. The B.R.D. Council offering to pay the sum of twopence for each rat caught during March. Also, sparrows the sum of 1/2d for each bird caught.

Cratfield resident prevented from going off the rails

10th June 1940

Derrick Girling: an application was received to place a railway carriage on his allotment. After some discussion it was decided to refuse application.

No go area in Spong Lane

February 27TH, 1941

Complaints had been made about the Chapel end of Spong Lane being flooded after rains. The Clerk was instructed to write to the area surveyor calling his attention and asking him to hurry to get the matter put right as motorists and the public were unable to get through.

Dig for victory!

April 21, 1941

Mr F. Mills tenant of Town Farm has been notified by the W.A. Committee that he has to break up by June 30th two meadows, one 2.444 acres, one 1.629 acres, for crops to be grown for the harvest of 1945.

Don't you know there's a war on?

November 13th, 1944

Was it possible to have the water piped in the village? Also to keep the children away from the windmill. It was decided to wait to see what happens at the end of the war.

Support your local team

October 10th, 1949

Clerk reported that the boys of the parish had asked if football sports gear be supplied. Mr Jallat would see if there was any fund that would help provide the gear.

Telecommunications upgrade required

November 14th, 1947

Mr Algar spoke about the need for a telephone call box for the Silverley's Green area of Cratfield.

This would be a huge benefit to that part of the Parish as the nearest phone box is a mile away at the Post Office. This is very necessary as we have no Doctor in the place.

Proposed by Mrs. Priestly, seconded by Mr Algar, that the clerk write to the officer in charge of telephones in Colchester to see what could be done.

Crying in the Chapel?

Congregational chapel.

The clerk was asked to find out which body of people were responsible for the chapel and to write suggesting that some action should be taken to prevent it becoming an eyesore in the village.

Bring back '**The Bell**'

13th January 1959

Bell Inn

The clerk was asked to write to Lacons Brewers, Yarmouth, to point out that the inn is one of the amenities of the village and to suggest that it should not be allowed to become dilapidated but, if possible, that it should be brought up to date or replaced with a new one. The Village loses a place round which much of its social life centres.

Creaking mill menace

23rd June 1959

Water Mills

A complaint has been made to the clerk and the chairman that nuisance was created when the water mill at Silverley's Green creaked in the wind affecting many residents. This was due to a loose rod.

Cratfield long ago

The Cratfield Papers 1490 - 1642 by **W Holland** give many insights into local records of Cratfield long ago. Here are some snippets.

1538 -39

Bill paid to Master Everard of Linstead Magna for a bow and arrows 3 shillings and 6 pence. Every Englishman and Irishman dwelling in England had been commanded by an act of Parliament passed 1466 to have a longbow of his own height. It was directed that butts should be made in every township.

1553

Sweating sickness found its way to Cratfield in 1553. There were 15 burials

'Who so ever was seized with the sickness died within 10 hours.' Some of the names of the victims were: Miles, Fisk, Orford, Thirkettle and Green. Some recognisably local names there!

1557

In this year in the adjoining village John Noyes was burnt at the stake.

'And so, he yielded up his life and when the body was taken down, they found one foot whole up to the ankle with the hose they buried it with him.'

1588

It [fee] payable to Richard Smythe of carrying the armour to Dunwyche.

It [fee] payable for a quarter of gun powder to Snape for the souldgers [soldiers].

1604

Paid Cady's wife for washing the town linen and making napkins for the communion table.

1066 and all that

Cratfield houses

Domesday Book

The Domesday Book tells us that in 1066 the Lord of Cratfield was the Saxon Thorth, son of Ufkil. By 1086 when the Domesday Book was produced the Lords were listed as Ralph Baynard and his nephew William Baynard. In 1100 Ralph's successor, Matilda de Liz, gave one-third of the manor to the Benedictine Priory of St Neots. During the Dissolution of the Monasteries under Henry VIII **Tithe Farm**, which had belonged to St Neots, was sold to a new lay owner – who had the right to collect the tithes – taxes which were originally paid to the Priory.

Some notable houses

Appleacre and the **Old Post Office** were originally one 16th century farmhouse dating from the sixteenth century. **Stokes Cottage** and **Bell End Cottage** were the barns belonging to the farmhouse.

The Bell Inn and Farm was an Inn for over three hundred years – from 1650 until it closed in 1959.

Bellevue was built around 1750 and was originally named **Dusts**. In the 1920s and 30s it was a tailor's shop.

Bell Green Corner Farm dates from the seventeenth century. In the 1980s it was the home of one on the smallest theatre in Britain, Somershey.

Tye Cottage was reputed to have been sold to the parish by John Tye in 1499. A Mrs James lived here for 40 years until she died, aged over

100 years.

The Old Thatched Cottage is one of the oldest houses in the village dating to around 1500.

Coppings, the old house in Tongs Lane, got its current name quite recently. It was derived from the maiden name of Catherine Sillett whose parents were the last to farm there. Before that it was called **Orchard Farm,** but the mediaeval name was **Tongs Farm**. Richard Tong lived there in 1327. Ivor Roberts-Jones lived here from 1971 to 1986. He was a sculptor. His statue of Winston Churchill, which was created in his barn, stands in Parliament Square London.

The Almshouse belonged to the parish until the 1960s. The building dates back to 1546 and was built by the parish at a cost of £25. 10. 3d

School Farm was a manor house and dates back to the 1500s.

Cratfield School was built in 1845 at the expense of the Rev Edmund Holland, who also built **Laxfield School**.

The Police House was built around 1936 as a new home to rehouse the village constable.

Stitchery

Images of over sixty of the old houses in Cratfield are depicted in a piece of stitchery completed in 2018 by Sue Eade and is on permanent display in St Mary's Church.

The Old Rectory and the Church
by Don Peacock
'a new, modern parsonage'

The economic realities of the twentieth century meant that like most rural villages Cratfield has to share a vicar with several neighbouring parishes. It is not a new problem, but it is an increasing one; fifty years ago, Cratfield was one of a group of three, at the millennium it was one of six and twenty years later it is one of eight. As a result, the Church found itself with more houses than it needed and in 2003, without a resident vicar, Cratfield vicarage shared the fate of so many others and was sold.

'...a perfect example of the late-Georgian vernacular...'

The original vicarage stood fifty yards or so to the north of the present site, on the other side of the pond. We can only guess at when or why it was replaced because the church records are missing but we can be certain that it was very different from the present house. What we see now is a perfect example of the late-Georgian vernacular; similar examples of the style in the village are Cratfield Lodge and The Manse. It would have been a fashionable choice as a replacement for its traditional timber framed predecessor. However, fashionable or not, there are signs that money was tight: using the pale gault brick, such as we see on Laxfield Baptist chapel or Cratfield Lodge, would have been smarter but considerably more expensive than the red brick that was chosen. Internally ceiling cornices were confined to two public rooms, joinery was all in painted softwood and ironmongery fittings were basic. But most telling of all is that as Suffolk parsonages go Cratfield is distinctly modest both in size and decoration.

'classical rules of proportion'

Despite the constraints, however, the vicar held on to the classical rules of proportion in ceiling heights, room sizes and door and window details throughout the building. He left another interesting hint in the garden as to his classical preferences by planting a dozen holm oaks, quercus ilex, a Mediterranean native much in favour in Renaissance Italy (they have flourished and are now two hundred year old giants).

A rectory – not a vicarage

The house is known as the Old Rectory but until recently Cratfield was always a vicarage. The difference is that traditionally it was the rector who received the income from the parish, the tithes, and if he was not resident, he paid a vicar to look after the congregation. So the hierarchy is clear. In Cratfield, when during the recent mergers the vicar of the parish also became rector of another parish in the benefice, he took the view that where the rector lives is a rectory - and so it remains.

The rector of a parish need not be an individual; it might be a monastery as was the case in Cratfield before the Reformation when the living was owned by a convent, St Neots. After the Dissolution it changed hands several times and it now belongs to a body called the Simeon Trust. The Rev Charles Simeon created the Trust for the express purpose of acquiring advowsons (the right to appoint vicars) to ensure that no vicar was appointed who might dilute the evangelical principles of the reformed church. Since the abolition of tithes the Simeon Trust can receive no income from the parish but it still has a say in the appointment of clergy.

'something of a scholar'

If it is not too fanciful, we might find clues to the character of the vicar responsible for the new house from the building choices he made. We could suggest that he was something of a scholar, certainly a modest man, probably confident and in starting from scratch with a new, modern parsonage undoubtedly energetic and optimistic for the future of the church. In fact, the sort of man likely to serve his parish well and of whom Rev Simeon would no doubt have approved.

Unfortunately, the church itself had been poorly served for some time and by the late nineteenth century it had fallen into such a ruinous state that it had to be closed for several years while major repairs were carried out. However, that was but another phase in the cycle of alternating care and neglect which the church has endured since its foundation. It may or may not continue but for the moment we can enjoy the fact that it is in as sound condition today as it has ever been.

Crime in St Mary's Church
The Reformation (1517-1648)

The rare and beautiful fifteenth Century seven sacramental font thought to be one of the finest in all England font was vandalised. Two of the panels are defaced.

1978

The four-hundred-year-old altar table was stolen in 1978. William Bailey, noted local builder and churchwarden, made another. He used wood that from an oak tree that had fallen in the churchyard and incorporated a piece that dropped from the original table and was kept in the vestry.

2016

Thieves were caught after it was discovered the lead had been stripped from one side of the church roof. To replace it cost just under £40,000. People were very generous, with donations concerts and fundraising. Soon the roof was repaired. Quick thinking locals spotted bits of clothing left behind by the thieves and handed them into the police who used DNA to make a successful arrest.

Cratfield's Notorious Murder

'...lying partly on a gooseberry bush ... her brains scattered in every direction...'

In 1793 a murder took place in Cratfield. The abhorrent nature of the unsolved crime made the Cratfield murder notorious all over the country.

Sometime between 6pm and 9pm On the 16th October 1793, Thomas Carter, a shopkeeper, and his daughter, Elizabeth, were brutally murdered with a hammer. At the trial witnesses stated that cries were heard that night and a single figure was seen running from the shop.

According to the trial documents the crime was discovered the following morning by:

'a woman who found the body of the female lying partly on a gooseberry bush in the garden fronting Carter's house, with her brains scattered in every direction, and the father was found murdered within the house.'

At the time of the murder no one had a clue as to who the perpetrator might have been. A series of coincidences led, many years later, to the arrest of 59-year-old Edmund Thrower, a blacksmith, who, years before, had made an alleged admission of guilt to an associate.

At his trial at Bury Assizes on March 2, 1812, Edmund Thrower admitted having attempted to rob the shop but alleged the murder had been done by his accomplices. Despite all the evidence being circumstantial and the fact that the crime had been committed 18 years previously, it took the jury only thirty-five minutes to find him guilty. He was hanged soon after, at Ipswich on March 23, 1812.

Local Recipes

Suffolk rusks

8oz self-raising flour

Pinch of salt

1 egg beaten

A little milk or water

Set oven to 450 F or mark 8. Sift the flour and salt together into a bowl then rub in the butter until it resembles bread crumbs. Stir in the beaten egg and enough milk or water to make a smooth dough. Roll out on a lightly floured board to about one inch in thickness then cut into 2 half rounds. Place on a greased baking sheet and cook for 10 mins. Remove from oven and split in half. Reduce the oven temperature to 375 F or mark 5. Return the rusks to the baking sheet cut side upwards and cook for a further 10 mins until crisp and brown.

Serve with butter and cheese.

Suffolk Dumplings

8oz flour

Pinch of salt

1/4pint cold water

Mix the flour and salt together then add the water mixing to form a firm dough.

Roll out 6 to 8 balls with floured hands then roll in a little extra flour. Put into a saucepan of fast boiling water cover and boil hard for 20 mins. Drain well and serve immediately with rich gravy as a starter or part of a main meal, or with melted butter or golden syrup as a dessert. A few currants can be added to the dough before boiling. Suffolk Dumplings, also known as Hard Dumplings, should be eaten with two forks being pulled apart to let out the steam.

CRATFIELD

Has changed with time.
Has seen the loss of
Crafts, cottages, the forge,
The shops, the village bus,
Carpenters, tailors, the village school.
Harness makers,
The place where workhorses were shod.
The pubs are lost
The sale of beers and wines
Restricted to a popup bar.

Yet at the bottom of the hill
The trickling Blythe meanders still
St Marys Church still scrapes the sky.

You look up and heave a sigh –
Most things have changed –
It's oh so true.
Time brings change –
So much that's lost,
So much that's new.

Take heed
For one day
You'll change too.

Chrissie Kitchen

PRODUCTION

Communications, interviews and research **Chrissie Kitchen**

Editing and advice **Nigel Cousins**

Printer **Leiston Press**

ACKNOWLEDGEMENTS

Julian Askew
John and Pam Brown
Robin Bryenton
Brian and Gwendoline Cole
Ralph Creasey
Tracy Eaton
Ted Greenard
Heather Hargood
Donny High
Lesley King
Don Peacock
Tubby Revell
Shirley Symonds
Roy Vincent
Tom and Sheila Webster

for their valuable time, loan of photographs and books

Photographs by kind permission

Pam Brown and Dave Eagling